As the Birds Land

A co-creation from

Laura Beckingham and

The Muse

Copyright © 2021 Laura Beckingham.

All rights reserved. No part of this publication may be reproduced, distributed, or transmitted in any form or by any means, including photocopying, recording, or other electronic or mechanical methods, without the prior written permission of the publisher, except in the case of brief quotations embodied in critical reviews and certain other noncommercial uses permitted by copyright law. For permission requests, write to the publisher, addressed "Attention: Permissions Coordinator," at the email address below.

Any references to historical events, real people, or real places are used fictitiously. Names, characters, and places are products of the author's imagination.

Cover image by Suzanne Waters (suzannewatersdesign.com)
Book design by Phil Bennett (pip-creative.com)

First printing edition 2021.

Self-published by Laura Beckingham
laura@spacewith-in.com
spacewith-in.com

As the Birds Land

*For those who came before me,
and those who walk with me now*

Foreword

'I think I must have been a bird once, I love the sky so much'

I first officially met the energy of The Muse in summer 2019. On writing retreat in Ireland, we were exploring the land, connecting with spirit, and sinking deep into magic and myth. We spent a day in Kilkenny, a place where some of my ancestors originate from. That day, just like the others, we wrote creatively to prompts. In the grounds of the castle, I wrote lots of pieces intuitively as always, but this time there was something different about them.

My teacher told me she recognised the voice I was writing in, as she had heard it come through me before. I knew that was true. A pattern seemed to be emerging.

I came home to London and kept writing but didn't think too much of it. Months later I was a delegate in a group 'Systemic Consciousness' programme. We spent a long weekend exploring the energies of the bigger societal and global systems to which we all belong, and how that was connected to our own personal inner and outer work in the world. During the night, after day one, I woke in my bed to the sound of a woman crying. I could hear her breath and feel her heartbroken sobs in my body as if they were my own. There was nobody there. I felt some words burning inside me, which wouldn't let me rest, so I got up, wrote them down quickly, and went back to sleep. The next morning, I read them:

'Those tears that wake you crying in the deepest part of night, they are yours, don't you know? And they are hers - all of them. For all of them'

'She is you. You are her'

I very clearly felt the message – there were ancient stories about things that happened hundreds of years ago that wanted to be told. I was being brought into contact with the energy of these stories and my job was to bring them forward so that the people who needed to hear them now, could. It felt weird, exciting, terrifying, powerful. More than anything it felt essential. So, I agreed to surrender, and the words started to flow through me, at pace.

As I captured and cultivated what showed up, I looked back and began to realise I had been writing with the energy of The Muse for years. Pieces I thought were poems or simply musings and even fiction were actually messages from her, or more accurately messages she and I had written together - her old wisdom coming through me in new ways. I spent lots of time visiting the river Thames in West London where I live, the river that's seen it all – the birth of modern-day capitalism, the rise of the patriarchy, the death of alchemy. The river that knows all the secrets and holds so much insight and truth. For months I went to the river daily and I would ask The Muse to join me - sitting on a bench with her for tea. We would talk to the birds, and to each other. I learned how to access the portal and draw wisdom from the well.

I remembered my Astrologer in Australia once telling me years earlier 'you can't leave the river until you've written the book'.

So, I kept going. Sensing her energy alongside me, and learning to understand what it represented enabled me to write and flow with ease –

stories and messages I knew were ancient and yet deeply relevant to our current times. I would look East, up the river towards Westminster, The City of London and onward to Canary Wharf where many of my clients in my business Space With-In work in fast-moving, complex commercial business and know that I was gathering things that they needed to hear. The birds kept coming, the portal grew deeper and more potent.

Somewhere along the line I was given the year 1571.

I started working with a teacher in America. One day I told him about The Muse. He told me things about her that he couldn't have known unless he knew her. He told me about the other people he knew who were connected with her energy too. Suddenly I discovered a whole web of us, weaving with her and energies like hers in different ways, all over the world. I learned in a constellation that in the late 1500s, when the wise women, the witches, were made to go inside and take human form to save their lives, that their magic was given to the birds, who were tasked with keeping it safe. I learned that I, a wise woman back then, had been stitched inside a bird too. I saw that the birds are ready to bring back the magic now, in a time where it is desperately needed - and they are looking for safe places to land.

So, these stories, this collection, this book are that. Old wisdom, being brought forward so it can be reimagined in new ways. The stories speak of the intelligence of the land and the wisdom of the body, the dogmatic aspect of religion, the oppressive nature of political systems, unhealthy masculine energy, abuse of power, misuse of wealth, and the fear of the deep and ancient intuition that runs through all of life. They are stories of what happened then, what was seen, heard and known. Stories of what was silenced, why and how.

These energies and stories simply want to be seen and heard - given their place in this story of life and carried forward into now. In bringing them together, we are being asked to listen and look, to gather and to reimagine the wisdom contained in them in new ways. We are being called to alchemise it for what's needed now, because things are the same but different, everything and nothing has changed.

The questions that mattered then matter now. They invite us to continue finding our voices and taking action for better balance in a world that needs it more than ever.

So, though this is ancient, poetic, somewhat mystical work it is actually a deep contemporary call to bring better balance to the way we lead and live today, so we can live more freely and leave a better world for those that come after us too.

The birds are landing. A new day is dawning. And this collection from me and The Muse can be a companion to guide your place in that. Please use it well.

(*The stories contained in this book refer, amongst other things to topics and experiences of sexual abuse, violence, suicide, ecocide. Please take care as you navigate your way and seek support as required).

Prologue

I was pulled towards that place and I never knew why, until one day it dawned on me that I'd been going there my whole life, in one form or another.

Going there, in fact for lifetimes, to that tiny faded spot there on the river banks underneath the mighty oak that I'd first saw take seed all those moons ago.

'You can't leave the river until you've written the book' she said to me - pulling the eight of wands from her tarot.

So I decided to stay. Decided to let it pull me, day after day, calling me in like a long silk thread that holds the secrets to all the lives I've lived and taken.

It's the birds I'm most drawn to at the moment. They've told me they are the keepers of the magic that was split from the witches when they were forced inside and made to take human form.

There's a bench there now and so I make my way there daily, to feed me.

They are looking for a place to land.

Contents

A Crow Stitching

The House of the Dark One
A Blood Portal
Steel Lungs
Inferno

Keepers of the Ways
Waters and Wind
Inspirited Earth
Kith and Kin

Weavers Weaving
Thread, Jars and Ribbons
Silver Apple Branches

A Crow Stitching

§

The year is 1571. I am just a girl in their eyes, but I know a lot.

I am a woman who sees everything. Especially the things that can't or aren't allowed to be seen or known. And certainly not shared.

I know rivers and forest and hedgerows. I know herbs and birds and fires. I am birds. And skies. I am roots and hollows. A cave. An answer, a searching.

Mostly I know him. His ways. His eyes. His mind. His soul. The very bones of him, enough to make and to destroy the very fabric of all being.

And he knows it. I know way too much. In fact, I know it all, even the things he daren't breathe out loud as a simple whisper and that's why one day soon they'll try to take me for it. They'll try to catch me for it, try to tame me, cage me, hang me, burn me, but I'll survive. For the truth and deep wisdom are fearless, endless - and live on beyond any body or being.

I will become the bird, in the sky where they can't find me. I will keep it all safe for us and one day I'll come back to land.

The House of the Dark One

A Blood Portal

Steel Lungs

Inferno

The House of the Dark One

A Blood Portal

§

She sits on a fence of her own making

Suddenly the wind starts whipping

In the field outside, a child screams into the distance

She doesn't know if it's hers or her.

§

There is so much rain. I've waited for days and days and felt the air get frozen, yet it still has not turned to snow as they promised it would.

I turn my face to the window to feel if I can feel it coming, lifting my eyes to the sky to see it.

Smell it.
Taste it.
Nothing.

In the distance, I hear a drum beat, softly. Messages carried on the wind from a distant land, to me, trapped here in the waiting.

I catch the resonance of them in my throat and swallow their stories down. When they said the snow was coming, I had thought they meant the weather, but the taste of salt and iron on my lips tells me it is death that will come marching.

I know all too well the flavour of this winter.

§

There is something to be learned here in the darkness of early morning. The shadows and the senses write a different story at this time.

§

It is spring.

The air is quiet, save for the sound of elderflower swaying in the wind - the wisps of its cotton falling all around me. I touch them with my fingers, bone weary, thin and brittle they offer little comfort - soft to the eye, poison to the touch, like so much of this broken landscape.

A crow calls. A sudden breath in has them scratching and all knowing at my throat, so bruised. I hadn't realised the choking would cut so deep, not there anyway - bleeding only tells half the story.

§

The blood bath remained after battle. Death and loss, vitriol, and venom - soaking the soil, seeping into the earth, flooding its vessels - contaminating everything that birthed and grew and lived there ever since.

Centuries old blood and bone and bile composted into every breath, every step, and every bite thereafter.

So, it's no wonder he was a monster, because death and loss and vitriol and venom were all he ever knew.

Then, as he turned eighteen and became the man the land had always destined him to be - is it any wonder he slit her throat - for in his heart, her warm life dripping through his fingers was the only thing that could keep him loyal and connected to the fathers from which he came.

§

There is no red in this land. Berries are purple, roses crimson, sunsets burned orange. All shades of nearly - and to the untrained eye, reds of sorts, but not to me. There is no red. No red. No red like the shape of our lust at the peak, no red like the way my heart beats for you, no red like the shame of not knowing. No red like the mess I made on my dress that day, walking home from the garden. No red like my face when I caught the neighbours staring. No red like the medicine they made me take for it. And no red like the pitch of her scream when I told her.

§

That war devoured the land, like it had each and every season past and would for every one thereafter.

The months when the rain came were always the hardest.

The barren bones of winter and the scorching summer sun had nothing on the times where we marched to our deaths through stinking, putrid bogland. Lush fertile soil quickly turns to quicksand when a thousand iron guts are spilled into it, and the stench and clag of spleen and bile can enfold you and pull you in like nothing you've ever known - feet first, until you die drowning in your dead brother's arms.

So I prayed for the start of the dry season, for my shattered kin to fade in to the freezing earth, to feed and seed the soil so we could feast again come spring.

§

To say that love is beautiful is only half the story.

I am waiting for them, and they are making their way here from the distance.

I am still. My hips ache and my knees scrape the floor.

It is cold.

To look at me I am resting. Inside I am all sharp edges, and it stings.

Waiting is harsh and pointed. Wanting is a gilded cage that knows no limits. Sweet things make you fat and I'd sooner split my heart open and eat it whole than put it on your table.

They are drawing close. I am still sat here waiting. Waiting. Waiting. Now I can see their faces it is all I can think of, and nothing is lovely anymore.

To say that love is beautiful is only half the story.

§

So long she had waited... moon after moon, as huge golden orbs faded to tiny silver slivers, then grew fat and round again... time after time.

She'd watched the seasons come and go: the brittle ground of winter softened by the first dust of snow. Vain yellow daffodils trumpeting proudly from the earth - suddenly overshadowed by the loud and boisterous song of sweet summer blossom.

She'd walked barefoot on confetti petals until they bled into the soil, and saw the farmers rip the bounty from the ground each and every harvest like a premature child taken early from its mother.

And then it would begin again, until years had passed this way... time after time.

So, this time when they came, she went eagerly, for she was hungry too - ravenous in fact - and now it was time to feast.

§

There are places I go to that no one else should ever know. Like benches on the river, where they visit, and whisper - their stories moving and living in my mind's eye.

Like the trees that line the banks, hidden corners under big old branches sheltering me as the secret rain falls down on all of them.

The night times, eyes wide, palms sweating, heart bleeding open, my body rigid.

The morning after he told me he'd slit his throat and burn the house down if she left him.

The dark corners of my mind when I see him do it.

The House of the Dark One

Steel Lungs

§

I wonder if they know that sat up here unnoticed under the cedar tree on the banks of the river, I can hear every word they whisper. They think it's safe to spill their secrets there on the water in the dead of night yet here I am scooping up every last one of them, tucking them safe and warm against my breast, every threat a thread I'll weave into the rope I'll use to choke them come morning.

§

It began to dawn on me that I had never really been welcome. That I am always held at arm's length, never truly fitting in.

Usually there is a man who makes it so, offering other women the graces he will barely afford to even consider for me. A false attempt at safety and a snare, drawing them all in. Reeling.

So, what is presented here is by no means new, for I have lived it in my bones for generations and it is soaked into the land upon which we walk and grow.

It is never safe for a woman to speak her truth. Never safe. Never safe for her to stand in the power of it, and certainly not for her to look him straight in the eye whilst she does it.

If she's lucky, a brave few will speak for her. A brave few will stand with her, whilst the majority look in the other direction or duck their heads for cover. Few will stand for you, even fewer will speak. The truth is that even the binders will fight to save their own skin. I do not need their sympathy, but I do crave their support, which I know will never come.

And make no mistake he will keep hunting, for the very essence of her story setting her free is the one that will burn down his houses and bring everything to its knees.

So I wish that I could say that this time it would be different. Wish I could know it will change. But they will die trying to hold on and take us down with them as they claw on to everything they have built, reaching for their power until their very last breath, simply handing it to their sons on the crossing over. They'd rather burn themselves with us than give any of it away.

§

Their story was complex. She had told me parts of it when I was very small in a way a mother always will - combing my hair by the fire and making me promise never to make the same mistakes that she did.

She told me how he'd found her. How he'd smiled his way in sweetly with her own mother, bringing wood for the fire and gifts for the table he'd taken her on too early and without consent that night as the family lay sleeping around them. She told me how he'd left the next morning without a word and with just a cursory glance at her mother, who had fed way more than his belly with the finest wares and let him take way more than he'd asked for, once again.

§

The wind surrounded them. Men. Men and dogs. Wolves. I have heard they live here, though I have never seen them in the waking hours. All of them a pack - still, but circling.

I sit far from them, but I wonder if they can catch my scent on the breeze - I do not know which way it blows today for it is mid-winter and the tides, winds and moods are always turning.

I am far enough away for them not to hear me - certainly not to see if I hide my face, and keep my head bowed low, eyes to the ground as they've taught me. From the shadows I can watch them and know that as I do that, they are blindly hunting me. My feet are pinned to the floor - I must leave but my legs have turned to stone and this time I cannot.

So, I turned back to look and every part of my body from my fingers to my toes wanted to run straight to them, screaming at the top of my voice, emptying my lungs of years of hate and poison, but I resisted, there is no one here to hear, no one but him, standing there, also frozen to the spot where his men and dogs had left him. I see his shadow before I see his form and icy breath on the wind, wisping its way to me. Words I'd share would just be wasted in his presence, for he is the only one bar me who knows the full story, and in words I've already whispered to him as he lay sleeping on the stone-cold bedroom floor last winter.

§

The waves found me, somehow.

I had sat there on that bench, quiet morning, day breaking softly, asking them, begging them not to visit. Turning my rosary over and over my tired, thin fingers - the spaces between prayer digging in bone like the breathless pause you hold when you know that someone dark is waiting.

It was in that moment I learned that the gap was the most fearsome thing of all.

The river swelled, a black, sudden, angry swell that told me they were coming. I listened to the wind - it said they were making their way here on horseback; I could hear them moving closely through the earth, my feet flat on the damp floor.

My body listened. Finally, I could breathe - a deep, moist sigh.

The beads fell from my lap into the freezing water, leaving me here. A penance in the waiting.

§

I visit him again.

He gets to be called a doctor, for a man who knows the ways of plants and the wisdom and worries of the body is a rare and cherished thing.

He is loved by the community, paid well, brought fine gifts and thanks aplenty.

Women who have this knowledge and more would sooner bite off their own tongue than share it. Imagine the power we could have if we were allowed to do our thing in public rather than talking in hushed voices on doorsteps and hearths, passing our potions to each other in the breadbasket.

Our very presence is a medicine, our breath a soothing tonic - that's a risky truth to own. That's a bitter pill to swallow.

§

I head down to the river to pray.

It is early morning, the time when days are long and the night passes through as merely a whisper.

The sound of bird song fills the air. The sky heavy and swollen with black, fit to bursting. My chest the same - heart and lungs too.

Nobody sees me. It's why I come so early. Those that do turn a blind eye for they know, as I do that this women's work is needed, and I do the same for them, gladly. To the untrained eye I am simply a woman going about her daily business. And that's exactly what I am - a woman going about her daily business. The business of bringing it all down, every single day. A dedication. A mission. A benediction. A crusade.

This is my pilgrimage. A path given to me (never chosen, but that I take freely) One I walk alone (to my knowledge, I swear there are others) and every step I make brings me closer to it. Brings me home.

Nobody sees me, as I kneel to tell the river, as I ask the cedar and the silver birch for blessing and give it all up to the wet that hangs in the air, soaking my hair and skin. As I tell the land to take him. As I ask the Earth to open up and devour him whole. As I promise to return tomorrow and the next day to make again this sacred blessing, for the rest of my days in this body if that's what's needed. Forever.

§

His presence was inescapable, all along this stretch of river. How could it not be, when you never knew who (or whether he) was watching?

Every rowing boat that passes in silence in the murky dead of night - every horse and cart, could be the vessel transporting him to his other worlds, where he can gouge and rape and beat any woman he pleased.

So that's why we bow and curtsy as the boat men pass

Why we tip our bonnets and flutter our eyes at every rider.

For sooner we be the shiny silver sixpence that catches his eye for treasure, than the dirty, rotten penny he carries in his breast pocket, to pay his whores for the next angry beggar he buys.

§

She ran through the flower beds and graves and hoped that no one saw her. Women like her weren't meant to come to places like this one, not alone and certainly not looking this way.

She had lost her bonnet. Not found it since the day he had pulled it from her as he grabbed at her hair, tossing her to the floor to rape her again. He wouldn't call it that of course – he'd simply say he was taking what was rightly his as he did in every other part of his life, because he could, even the law and God said so (or he told everyone they did at least).

I'd never been someone who'd taken to wearing a bonnet – smiling sweetly and fluttering my eyelashes is not for me, but today I wish I had it, for it may stop their eyes from seeing - the stone cold shape of my face and the look in my eye that said exactly what I had in mind to do next.

§

There is always a woman that turns. It is always, always the way.

Sometimes it happens in an instant. Most often these days it is a deeper, slower burn that rages from the inside out and cuts you off at your feet as you walk the world freely. The freer you get, the harder it stings. Holes are always made for falling.

There is no easy way to describe it. One day, as if from nowhere, the world simply turns, and everything is changed in an instant. From that place, nothing can ever be the same again - sadly, very sadly it is just so.

So, it is sad to be on the same side of this story once more, yet here I am, again. It is to do with attention I know - she simply cannot bear it, but I have no need to be the queen on the throne when I can be sovereign of my own underground castle. She covets his eyes, his smile, wants to know where they go and where they don't. In the movement between there is grabbing because she cannot take it. A loss of focus means the sky comes falling in, a darkness descends and most of what was known is lost, forever. A babe suckling at the breast does not guarantee a place here. Once again, I am blindsided, and most of my anger is directed at that, for I should know not to get caught napping and should've seen it come. I feel their heads turn toward me so quickly their necks could snap and their eyes on me now more than ever. Tonight when they are sleeping I shall crawl into their beds and take one from each of them - gather them up like shiny marbles in my silken pocket, make my way silently down my river to home, where I shall sit on the step in the soft light of morning stitching each of them into the back of my head with hair from the loom... I am the one who is watching now, and you are so blind you will never even see it.

§

You believe you have right of way.

And you are right in my way.

Every time you brush past me, caring not to even look at me, I see you.

What you don't see is me following you light-footed along the river. You don't see me trail in your wake pretending not to be there and following every footstep you take on your path home to assumed, untested safety.

I know where you live now, and I have taken shelter under the bough of the lime tree to watch you, foolishly at ease there. I know the route you walk so boldly every day, mid-morning. Know the places you pause to take rest in and the dark corners along the way that call me.

Today I walk the route without you. At dawn, tomorrow, the same and still nobody sees me. Nobody knows what I gather, nobody knows my plan.

§

The church bells ring in the distance, as they do every day at this time of morning. I never knew if they were calling me kindly to them or asking me to run as fast as my legs could carry me away, but today I am clear it is the latter, so I pick up my skirt and sprint down the lane.

I can hear his voice deep inside them – the further I go the louder it shouts me, the whisper under the peals morphing in to beating drums that climb inside the corners of my mind. My body aches for freedom – a true kind of freedom that deep inside my heart I know a woman like me will never know.

The crows are here again – their angry songs drown out his screams for just a moment. I pause for breath in the stillness. I am safe here for a moment. This I'll take for now.

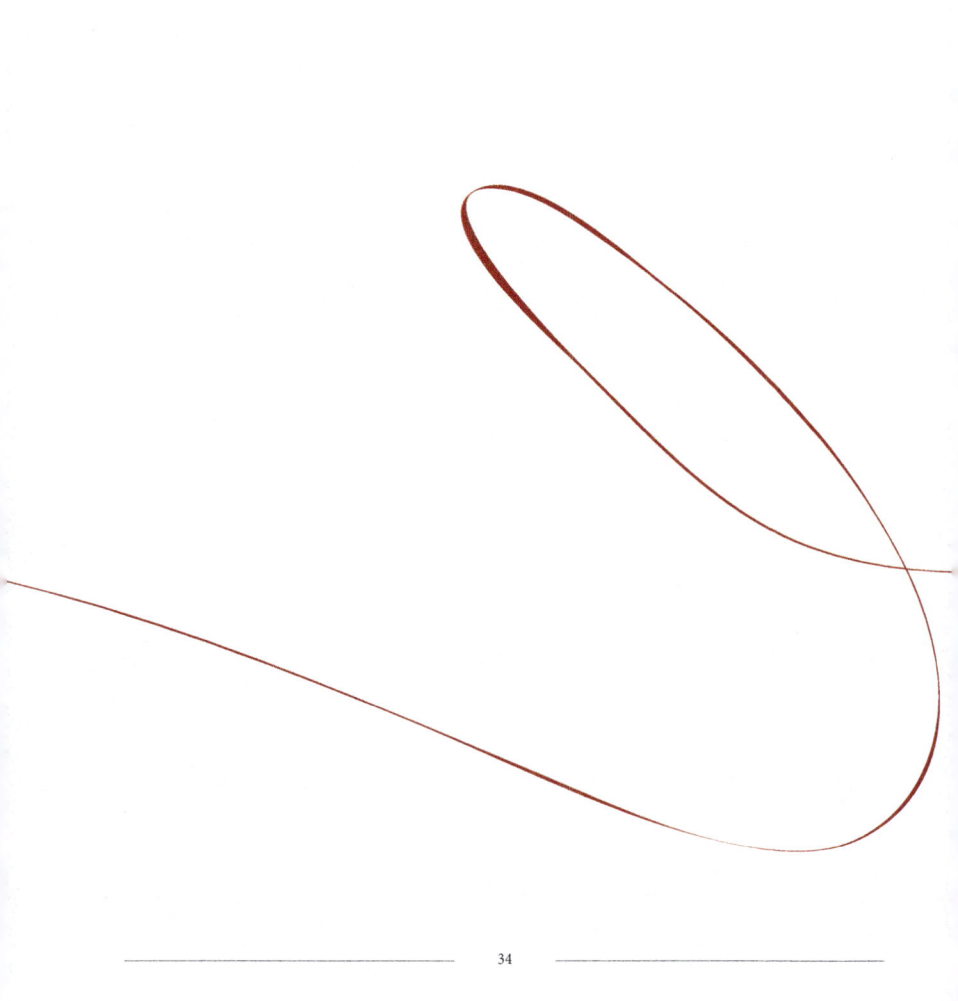

The House of the Dark One
Inferno

§

The man I've told you about, remember

The one who rapes and beats and pillages all with the ease of a man who knows how and thinks it's his birth right to do so:

Him

Well here he is, right in front of my eyes again.

I always promised myself that when this day came, I'd slit his huge, jowly lucid throat right open there and then, walk away and never look back

But I hadn't expected so many people to be here

Hadn't expected it to be broad, bright mid-summer light,

Hadn't expected the river, the children, the laughter

I'd dreamt of black dark and dampness, sour breath and salty tears and him climbing in the window like the cheap and dirty rapist he really was

I felt the pointed dagger tip in my pocket

Rubbed my tiny, bone-weary fingers over its truth

Sheathed it, again in a way I couldn't ever sheathe him

Looked up through fluttered eyelids

Gritted my teeth

Bit my tongue

And swallowed my rage whole. For now.

Bent to my knees in curtsy

Lifted my skirt, this time in greeting, not to get fucked

Looked him dead in the eyes and smiled.

You'll keep.

§

They speak of waiting for me as if I am not always watching and waiting for them - in the pitch-dark garden, silver keys in my pocket, turning red threads over and over the blood red veins on my hand, again and again.

It is the middle of the night. The door knocks and I let him in, smiling gently.

I am seething.

Once again, he stands before me a foolish, idle man professing to know all about things simply for the books he's read and the lists he has written, when I'm the one who's lived the life he only dares to speak of and he happily takes lessons from me every time he comes to visit.

He calls me his mistress. I am a secret other than to the whole world of men just like him, who he passes me around to so freely like a prize stallion taken out to breed.

What happens here is rape. What happened is this woman lured him in simply with the scent of her and now he believes I'm his for the taking so long as he wishes to buy.

I let my body surrender. It feels nothing anyway, not in his presence, and I slide out of myself, leaving it there, slipping silently under the door frame as I move gently back to the garden, where I watch myself getting fucked unwillingly again through the freshly glazed window he paid for.

The fire burns low, my spirit raging. I run the thin red thread over my finger, dig my nails in to the warm flesh of my skin and tie another knot for him.

§

I slip silently to my knees and look up to beg forgiveness from the Heavenly Father, who does nothing but watch silently from afar over the abuse doled out so freely by the ones he's chosen to represent and reign for him here on Earth.

Nothing, that is, except to grant them more power, day by day, year by year, watching them grow stronger and more entitled by the minute.

How can they call the Church a sanctuary when prayer bleeds my knees to the bone in the same way he does, night after night after night? The stone-cold floor offering little more comfort than the one he forces me to by my throat every time he calls to court me.

There is no safety here. No confessional that can wipe away the sins I have in mind, and no amount of candles that can light a path to his, or my redemption. He took my soul for his own years ago, ripping it from my gaping mouth and pissing all over it on the floor of his stinking bed chamber whilst I watched, wide-eyed in disbelief and horror.

Well now I am a believer, for I have nothing to lose, and there is nothing left to save - no sacredness remains in this empty vessel. So from this point I know there is no going back, only forward steps to be taken as I march firmly onward with steel lungs and unblinking eyes, straight into the heart of the inferno.

They say hell hath no fury like a woman scorned.

I say hell comes to you in female form, smiling sweetly.

And when you least expect it.

§

I went straight to the cave where the bone men sing. Sometimes they call me to them, sometimes it's simply a whisper on the wind - either way I go gladly, sliding into the warmth and darkness once again, the land wet under foot, the smell of silt in the air a tonic to my aching lungs and soul.

I go there to rest. Deep into the earth where life is just a memory and light cannot dare to show you what waits in the darkness. I go for the water, and I go to feed upon the rich salty earth and the shadows of the ancient ones who sat round the fire before me.

The cave is barely a shelter. To the naked eye it is nothing, but to the watcher it is a whole world of wonder, rooms within a room undiscovered, roads trodden and paths untaken.

I take my seat around the hearth, a ritual that has become familiar. I feel the warmth of their bodies next to mine, their breath on my skin, our hearts beating. I close my eyes and wait, breathing deeply. Pausing. Breathing. I push my feet into the soil, sinking my toes deep into the moist flesh of the earth, my fingers on my naked breast. I am ready. I beg for them to come, my breath shallow, body wanting, heaving and writhing as it will be until they arrive. There is pleasure in the waiting.

I cannot see them. I do not need to, for the stories they need to tell me move through my wanting body - ripples of pleasure like the touch of a man taking what's his and the deep throbbing pain of a child ripped from me too early, bitter iron blood spilling onto the rocks, in offering and sacrifice.

A thousand times I would do this and a thousand times more, for every chance is a miracle and every visit a blessing.

The wind rattles over the walls. The flames lighting the way blow cold and hollow. I feel them scuttle to the corners. The cave lies empty. Nothing and no one is here now, not even me. But I have what I need – still, I will come again tomorrow.

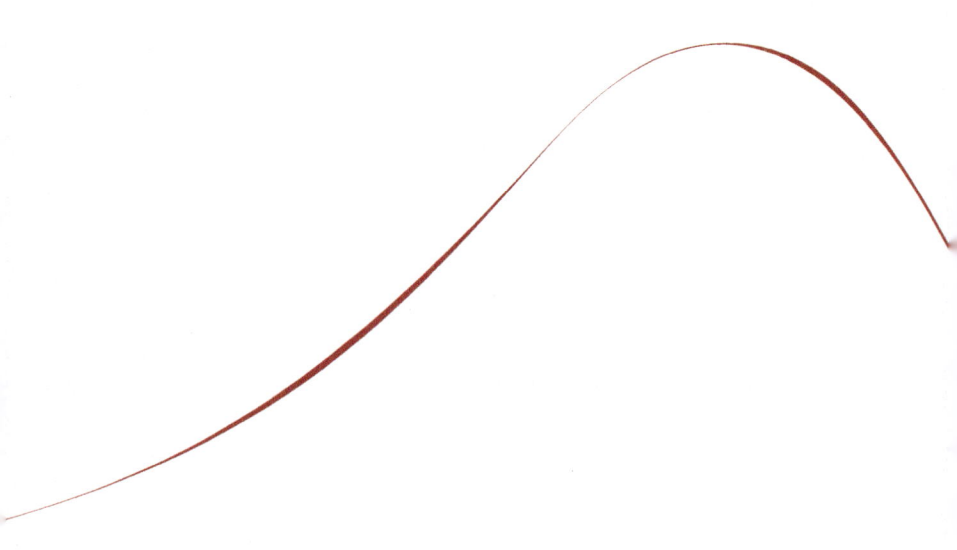

§

There will be ashes raining down on you from the fire fuelled sky to the scorched amber earth when I leave you.

And nothing will ever be the same again.

You asked me here to stoke the fire and fan the flames - but didn't you realise that in my tending and creation I bring destruction? For it is all I really know: an awakening and a changing of everything that ever was into something new, unrecognisable, warped and molten.

I. am. raw. power.

Unstoppable,

Unbreakable.

You cannot control me,

Cannot influence me,

Dare you even try, and I will melt you:

Solid to liquid,

Love to hate,

Blood to ash,

Bone to dust.

§

They tried to burn me - exhausted, I tried to fight them.

Then I realised that heat is simply sensation, and all sensation is life.

So, I climbed into the heart of the fire, and became the flame.

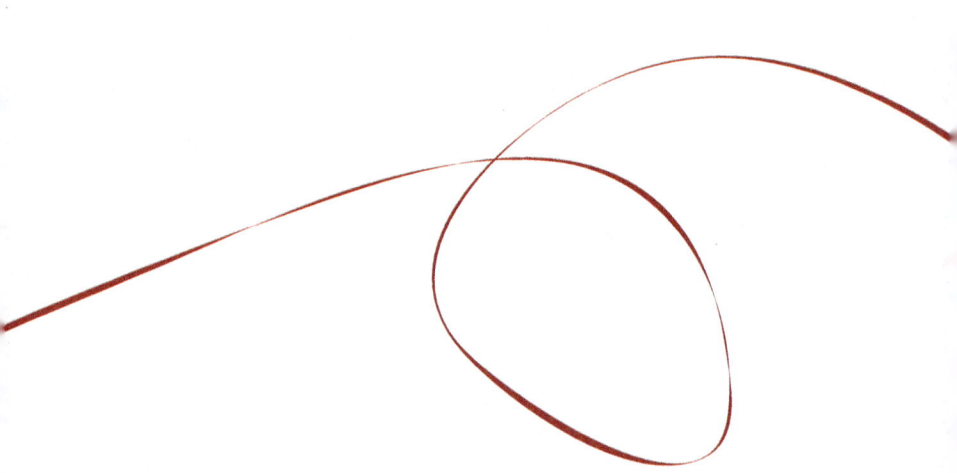

Keepers of the Ways

Waters and Wind

Inspirited Earth

Kith and Kin

Keepers of the Ways
Waters and Wind

§

She told me she knows how to listen to the river.

She says that she will teach me.

§

There is something quite unique about the darkness. How the stories come through in the shadows of the night.

Rain brings them to me, each drop a blessed footstep - each moment a thousand stories and ancestors come knocking at my door.

Some nights I sleep through and meet them in the dreamland. Most nights I rise to greet them at the witching hour - inviting them to sit with me, holding me through to the dawn.

§

The days I know are full of heavy skies and hard clouds hanging low - dark, dank, and waiting .

These are the ones I feel. These are the ones I remember.

§

The wind called. I am in the sky again - a watcher, moving and stillness, everything slow motion.

This is where it all unfolds.

I have been telling them forever that they need to give it to the river, and of course they do, but the bones of it need to go to the sky, and for them to know that I need to show them.

Down below me nobody is watching. I have never moved slow enough here to realise that this is the only place they cannot see. The wind moves my breath as I feel it. I swallow it down deeply - a belly full of sky, and make my way down to earth, slowly.

§

I am afraid that you will leave me if I stand still for too long. I look at the ground and lose you.

Fear isn't just my middle name.

I ask her to hold the sky for me - she does so, willingly, and I am here again, able to see now.

You tug at my clothing, but I can't turn to face you. This time, this needs attendance. I must wait.

I feel your breath at my neck, or maybe it's the autumn winds turning.

You'll be patient, I know, but not forever.

You tap me on the shoulder firmly, asking me to go with you.

I'm not ready.

You leave.

I stay.

§

Icy rain whipped through the air, the wind howling and above me a single bird sang sadly to the solemn sky.

The river is black. An angry swell. I wonder how many secrets it has taken to look this way and whether it has room for the one more I daren't tell.

The tide is leaving. There is a tunnel in the woods, and I'm scared to take it, for I have no idea where it leads, but I run to it swiftly - away from the truth of the river, deep into the truth of the land.

§

It felt like rain, and I thought I knew it, yet I find myself bizarrely unprepared in this deeply familiar, yet strange and unknown land.

I have been here before, but not this time. This storm isn't carving me open. The soil isn't wet to soaking in a way that it will open right up and swallow me whole, devouring every inch of who I am and what I know.

I was once afraid when the rain came to signal the start of the black and brittle season, and I had every right to be, for life hung by a thread then, delicately balanced, on a knife-edge over a crevice.

And now things are different.

(I can just let it soak my skin and be here now).

§

I could hear her singing and her breath so close to me I wasn't sure if it was the wind whistling though the window, or her cold face against my skin.

We are alone now. No voices whispering, no faces staring blankly through the window.

I find myself weeping, unfamiliar tears that belong to neither of us yet feel more real than anything I could ever imagine. I know I am weeping for the land and for everything it's born witness to. Weeping like the big old willow at the riverbanks bursting, and like the rain that comes so suddenly it soaks you to the skin leaving you so translucent they get to know you bone deep, your inside out sighing, whether you want them to or not.

§

I am always looking at the sky - not turning my face to the sun as most of them, but lifting my head to the clouds so the wind can take me.

I call it in - I have always known how to bring it. Once I tried to catch it in a jar, but it shattered in to a million pieces, and I know I would too if they tried to hold me.

It is my favourite time of year - tree bones fusing, the earth is damp underfoot and all days smell of mushrooms. The wind starts whipping in the distance - to others, nothing, but I can hear it all. The weather whispers to me, sharp and piercing, begging me to listen here at the cliff edge, forcing me to hear it scream.

§

She walked towards the water.

She'd been here a hundred times before - maybe thousands, day after day, moon after moon, forever. The more time passed, the less it meant a thing, like saying goodbye to old friends you'd never really known anyway. Even so, it felt fresh and new each morning, not in a light and warm 'what's possible' way, but in a way that invited her to step inside, submerge her skin and surrender to every shade of darkness.

That's why she kept coming back here, returning over and over despite what they said. Lately, she'd taken to arriving just before dawn so she could count the drops of silver on the surface as the jackdaws rose, and if lucky, slip a silver sixpence of them into her pocket for wish-making, later.

They didn't know that's why she came here of course, how could she tell them? She knew she'd be taken for it - locked away, perhaps tortured, even killed, but that wasn't the worst of it. What she feared most was the look on their faces when she told them what she was really there for - them mirroring back to her that the remembering was something they would never truly understand.

§

There was water and there were birds, as there often is, but this time everything about it felt different. I don't think I'd ever noticed the depth of the river, or the birds with their red faces and tiny, somewhat broken wings. I wonder what shame they have seen in these waters and how long it took them drinking it up for it to fill their bodies to the brim.

I bend to look at my own reflection, carefully, so as not to fall in, but mainly so not to turn my back in a way that one could push me. The current is strong, and I could easily go under. The water is moving, softly, wind blows over the truth of its edges and it takes some time to settle.

Staring back at me is her, and she is me. As I look, I remember them - all of these faces, the versions of me I have known and all the others in-between. Most would say they've never seen me this way - such is the way when you learn to slip off and on so many different skins.

For a moment, I am with her. I watch her, watching me. Memories come flooding - just like the water, of mothers and battles and fields, moons, and moments. The harvest. Waiting.

I stay a moment, try to catch the thread of it and tuck the ball of wool safely in to my breast pocket near my heart where it can settle like the water before the wind can take it.

There are stories to be found here in this river, and soon I will submerge myself into its water, back to where I came from to learn the truths of it. For now though, the thread, my open heart, the pocket, the memories, the waiting.

§

Those tears that wake you crying in the deepest part of night,
They are yours, don't you know? And they are hers - all of them.
For all of them.

A thousand stories, rolled over a thousand years, a thousand times in to this tiny, throat scratching, breath taking, salty drop that stirs you sweating and voiceless, a body shaking - heaving for the weight and the loss of the soul, all the souls it knows, yet has never truly met.

She is you.
You are her.
And these tears you cry silently are for the deaths of all the mothers. The rape of the land and its babies, the pain, the pain of the anger and the shame of the ones who bore it.

A thousand tears won't cry away the sins of his hand, won't (no matter how shiny) gloss over the truth, mask the stench of his hatred or hide the vile atrophy that spills from his veins, but they may start to fill the crevice he plundered.
So, cry enough.
Cry some more.
Breathe, let them pour, let them rain.

Let them reign, and the huge wide open fractured wound ripping through the curves of your land will fill and fill to bursting.

Saltwater births a thousand blessings. Your tears the bounty, the deep lake of life and wonder.

And you,

You carry every drop with you.

For you, are the river.

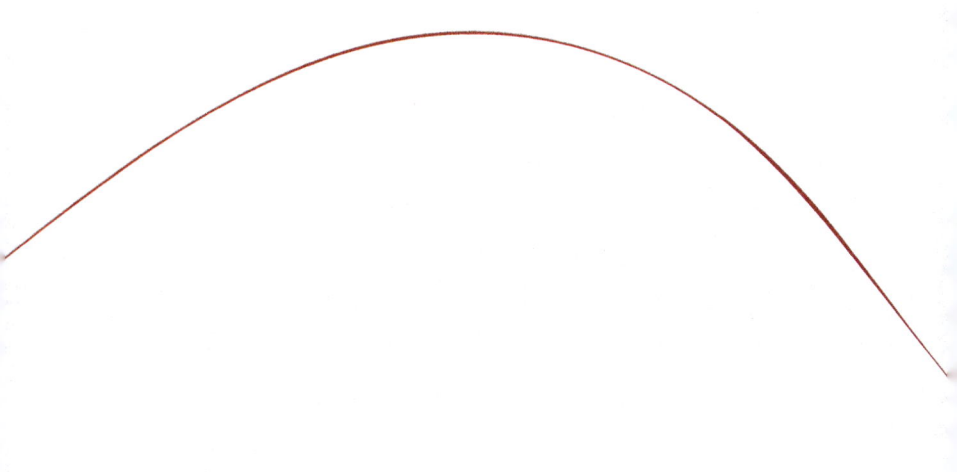

§

There will be rain
And there will be waiting
When I leave you there
Watching
And waiting.

I will lift my head to the sky
Hear it coming
Know that it's time.

I cannot change this
And I am settling
But there will still be rain.
And there will always be waiting.

§

I turn my face up to the sky

Take a wide, courageous breath

And whisper to my heart

'Soften now

Open

Tear open.

And make it sacred.'

Keepers of the Ways

Inspirited Earth

§

There is a message in this land, but they cannot hear it, and they never will, for they do not know how to listen.

§

I could smell the elements.

The damp, cool wind a mix of earth, water, and air. And the sun on my face bouncing in dappled light from the ferns outside my window.

Hot pins pricked my skin. Some a memory, some an idea, most a promise - for which I am waiting.

The sudden sound of birds spun me from my daydream. I don't know what or where they are but there are many and lately, they have visited every morning.

Reluctantly I open my eyes. At this moment I realise I know nothing. But I do know my body. I do know the land. And I do know that I am waiting.

§

It was a wild day. It seemed the depths of autumn when really it was the peak of spring. Thick blankets of leaves tangled my feet and I wondered if overnight the world had actually turned on its head without anyone realising.

There's a big old lime tree on the path to the river and I made my way hurriedly to it to take shelter. I will wait there. I will ask them to visit. Call them in to share my secrets. Some may come, most daren't and that's enough, for now.

The trees will listen under the wind, they always do, and earth can take it all.

§

The snow has been falling, it is as delicate as lace - somewhat late for the season and warmly welcomed, nonetheless.

I knew this would happen, for I saw it coming as I always do - I have long had a way with the weather and my mother said I was brought to her on the wind in April showers, so when the sky cries, I feel it is calling to me.

Lately I have taken to rising early. Dawn is my favourite time and yet today I have woken slightly later - the snow there to greet me. I shall feign surprise, when I see it.

I find myself heading to the river - he has said he will come with me so I let him, but I know that I will leave him halfway even if I must slip out of my skin to do it as I so often do.

We make our way there, the ground soft underfoot just as I like it, clouds above us heavy in an opaque sky, the birds watching from overhead as always.

I see them looking a different way this morning, but I have learned to always listen, so I go, kissing him lightly on the cheek and smiling gently as I do so.

I walk along the river - this is a path I have taken many times - I come here almost daily, a pilgrimage of sorts, but there is something strange about the air this day. Snow has a way of weaving a veil that nothing else is able and I wonder what will be there when I lift it. Somehow, I am never able to quite see through.

The woods are the right place for me to be now, silver birch and willow that know how to bend and move with the same wind that brought me. The ground is stirring, the curtain drawing thin. These trees have ears for listening and know all the stories of this land - they have said they will come to take them and I cannot bear to hear it, so today I will simply sit with them, crafting a web with the thread I keep deep inside my pocket - I will stitch all day and night if I have to, lying on the frozen floor, laying my heart face down on the earth to warm its bones with mine.

Nothing will stop me. Nothing will let them take it from us - that is my eternal promise.

§

The owl, she is back. She comes to visit more often, after that first time at dusk on Winter Solstice, the shortest day. Every call from her is an invitation to enter a third dimension. Every call to me is one I answer gladly.

Today she takes me to the cave. I have been here before, but not in this way - this time I am the one tending the fire. It burns low - a subtle ember, warm, not blazing but enough to warm our hearts and light the path for those still coming. Last time I was here I heard the bone men sing, but this time it's the earth that cries out to me, asking me to lie down low, begging me to let go and listen.

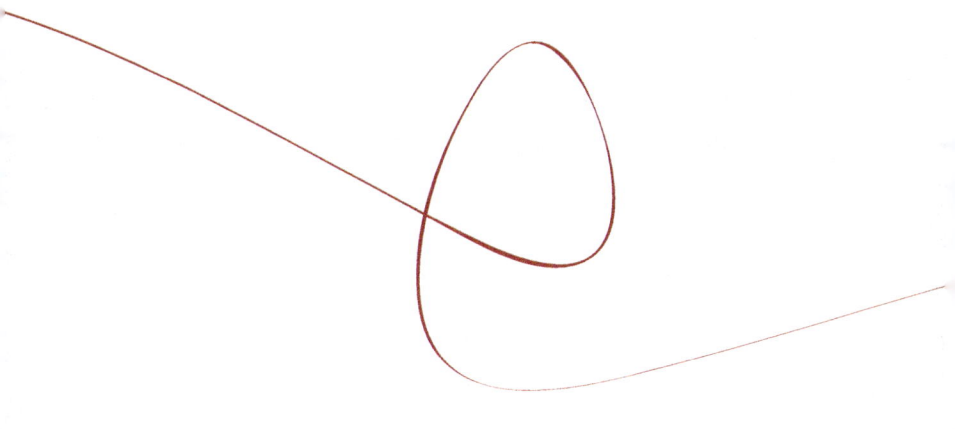

§

I know these trees. They have been here since I was a girl and for many more moons longer.

Mostly, I know the land they stand upon, and the earth they bury their roots in so deeply like I do every night when I peel back the rug under my feet, open the trap door of my heart and slide down into the core of it, resting there gently until morning.

As I pass them at dawn, I know they know this. They see a piece of me that no one else will. They smell the dirt and the mushrooms soaked in to my skin, even when I have washed it down and dowsed myself with lavender.

I am made for forest floors over freshly mown fields.

§

They say that a new day is dawning and though my mind knows it should be true, my body tells a different story and I have always trusted my heart when it comes to these matters.

They speak of an uprising, and every morning I put my feet firmly on the floor, longing to feel their distant march beat through them, but as yet it has not come.

The heart you see, tells a truer story. One we rarely listen to - one we do not want to hear.

§

I march swiftly to the water well as if my life depended on it, for it does and I do.

I strip my clothes off - naked is the only way and sooner I be hung dead for that than what else they would accuse me of. I fold my shift neatly and tuck it to one side under the shade of the big old oak I played in when I was a girl.

Squatting over the gape of it, I sniff the damp air from the well right in to my lungs. They'd call me deranged if they saw it - at worst a monster but to me it is delicious.

Unfolding my long legs from under me I place one foot firmly on each side of the wall, one hand too. This is how I get down there. I say farewell to the light and slide down the wet walls, delighting at the rough and slippy feel of it, green and moist against my skin.

They say I am a witch, but I don't come here to make magic, I am hungry, for the truth of the earth - the wisdom of the land, and I come here to feed.

§

I've learned to listen to these lands, though I was not born to them. Mother says I was brought to her on the wind, falling one day from a stormy sky into her arms - a winter blessing.

Deep in the heart of the forest I would play when I was young - I went to see the trees and could never find my way home because the land was always moving. I told them I had fallen or gotten waylaid, which I had of course, but not in the way they imagined. Most people believe the earth to be still, and I know that's never true because I feel it, and they told me.

There is a tunnel in the woods, and I don't know how long it's been there - one day soon I'm going to return to it and see how to find my way in. I've been waiting for the call to go deep into the bowels of the earth and feel it from the inside out. I know its heartbeat as a pleasure running through me, like it could eat me, or given the chance, like I could devour it whole.

§

I am all of it, and you are all of me.

Us, all of them.

Everyone who ever walked before us and every path they walked it on. Every step taken, every bone, every tear, wrapped layer upon layer, silk and soil to this very day - a prayer for the living whispered on their dying breaths, taken by the wind, ridden over the seas and right back every day in every storm that touches your heart and every sun that shines for you.

I take my mother's hand in mine. I feel my grandmother on her fingertips, imprinted bone-deep, a whisper, a memory, a knowing.

In this body I am living, in this land I am home.

Keepers of the Ways

Kith and Kin

§

My job is to collect the water, clean the space, lay the fire, light it. Invite the people, fill the pot, boil the pot, and wait.

We gather. Many join, some just briefly, most stay, others won't. There are those who come every time they're called to and there is always someone new. All are welcome. We sit in circle, open the doors to our hearts, we drink the medicine - and listen.

This is how it begins.

§

She is here to warn me of the danger.

Normally I wouldn't open the door to a wizened old woman like her - but one day soon she'll be me, so this time I do.

She knows.

We go straight to the truth and speak of it all - of the land and its knowing, of the river and what it's seen. She tells me of plants and their uses, how to work under the light of the moon and listen to the rhythm of the fields and the forest. She wants to take me there, deep in to the woods to sit with the trees on the longest day, to talk to the spirits and learn the magic of it all. We'll tie ribbons on branches, drink from the well and give our wishes and wants to the water. Leaving there we'll fill a basket and when they ask us, we'll say we were gathering wood for the fire and lost our way. They'll smile, a forced smile of course and make a note in a pocketbook so someone can come with us next time, for safety.

I pour a warm ale with the herbs I grow right here in the garden. She drinks it. She makes me promise never to write any of it down but to pass the message only through tongues as she does, in dark corners, around fires like mine. She tells me of the many women like us, keepers of wisdom, guardians of it all, but she will not say their names. She will never say mine and by dawn they'll take her for it - the men she warns me of, who march long days to find us.

Deep in to night I am exhausted. I want to stay but I cannot for though I've always known, to speak of this so freely brings a different form of slumber. I must sleep. Secrets that can't make words have nowhere to go but to our bones and that needs rest for making.

She says she will call again tomorrow.

Sun rises. I wait in, walking sometimes to the gate in the garden, my eyes soft but searching until the darkness comes. Same again the next night and the next. The fire burns ever lower. The knock never comes.

§

Winter is not coming. It is already here. Heavy snow comes down outside my window. It is nightfall - the light has all but gone and I do not know if I will make it home in time.

I have been told I must get to the top in every season, especially this one - but every time I try to do so there is something blocking my path. I keep trying. Even this story doesn't quite want to be written. This is a time for patience.

Someone has taken my shoes. The feel of the feet touching the earth seems to be the point of this story - the path and the crescendo. And to be witnessed doing it is what it's all about this time - to know that despite the pain there is pleasure in this story - this is why we keep going despite the rocks in our path. There are others and they need to know this. I can show them, and she can be there to guide me.

§

Sing me your song.

Come to me in the night and find me. Meet me in the waiting.

Breathe with me under the light of a full ripe moon, your mouth at my breast, wanting.

Howl, wide-open. Swallow me whole and more, skin on skin. Consume me.

Know me inside and out, a story. Ask questions with no answers.

Stay.

§

When she speaks, the voices of a thousand women fill the room and break the silence. I don't know if she's called them here or I have - we have, but they keep coming and I sense there are more.

They are praying. A gentle rhythmic song that touches me deeply in this quiet. An offering and an ask, I can't tell if it's of joy, hope or sadness - perhaps it's all of them and more, as in this life that we are living. They pray for us who wake for them, and their song fills the spaces between us like nothing else can.

We are gathered here in circle - they say she is a medicine woman - that she can soothe you to a slumber in ten beats of your heart, but tonight mine is racing. There is a threshold to be crossed here, a bridge between worlds, a beckoning, and an invitation.

They wait - and we are walking to them.

§

I came to see you today and sat in a different place because I wonder if you have new things to tell me, and she said there was more that you wanted to share.

It's been snowing. I think you and the weather are allies. Perhaps you even are the weather, for I feel you most often on the wind and you come to me more deeply in the biting damp of the dark season.

I know these riverbanks are yours - and every tide brings a story, each turning both a new and old page, but I wonder - with whom else did you travel and where, oh where did they take you?

§

There are Monks. They sing a solemn song, perhaps for me, perhaps for their brothers.

It is prayerful - a mourning, both of what's gone and what's surely coming.

There is so much beauty. As the men sing, the women gather. They fill their lungs. We fill our cups. They light their candles, we sit in darkness, still in silence - building our own ring of fire.

§

There was a day that she didn't show, and I knew before the knock came, deep in the heart of my belly that she was gone.

Gone from the village.
Gone from her body.
Gone from me, perhaps. For now.

I shut myself in the room with no windows and cried for hours - heaving, wracking, sobbing tears that I imagine one should shed for a mother, if she'd had one.

I couldn't tell a soul - nobody was ever to know of us, she'd made me promise and keeping my word was the last thing I could do to honour her, so I stitched my lips closed again and swallowed my tongue whole.

I let the grief ride through me like a wave. I swam in it, drowned in it. I rode it like a horse, galloped it all the way to the woods and found a safe spot next to a big old oak tree she'd shown me. There, under the shade of the ancient branches, I pulled it all out of my body from the guts up, ate some, put the rest of it in a jar, sealed it with broken waxes and buried it deep into the ground I stood on.

I will return for it later.

Weavers Weaving

Threads, Jars and Ribbons

Silver Apple Branches

Weavers Weaving
Thread, Jars and Ribbons

§

He has told me I must share the stories, and though I have waited a lifetime for a man to see me and them like this, I am absolutely terrified.

I do not know how to do it, but I do know he is right. If I don't share them - and soon, the riverbanks will burst, and the land will simply not be able to take it. All will be lost, I can feel that - my head aches so badly with the truth of it and this morning on the boat crossing I heard the water tell me too. It knows everything there is to know of nothingness and darkling - I have always trusted that.

It is a strange day to receive this message - soft, slow, and dappled in the light of early spring sunshine. I am sitting by the fire, watching the garden when it comes. I always imagined that when it happened there would be thunderstorms and lightening, or that perhaps the earth would open up and try to swallow me whole, but it turns out that despite the biting cold it was nothing more than a gentle breeze - merely a whisper on the wind, coming in quietly from across the sea.

So I am terrified, and I am ready. Very ready.

I have no idea where to begin, but for now I can clear a space and make ready for the coming. I can pull in threads from everything I've gathered, light a flame, and tie a ribbon. I can set the bluebird free and slip into darker bones and skin. I can begin again - and I know fine well how to do that.

§

I know I am afraid to walk this line, for I fear with every step I take I might cross it.

That's why I walk it so tenderly, hiding the bones of it inside my prayer book and under the folds of my skirt.

But walk it I do, and every time you see me pausing fear not - I am not waiting for permission, or an invitation, I am gathering - stones in my pockets, allies for the journey and enough energy for us to fight our way home.

§

Though time trudged on I could feel it was the break of winter and spring was on its way.

These days have been hard. Never have I marched so fully into the bosom of the season, but short days, long nights, incessant dampness, and the stench of plague had me breaking free from my confinement, longing to dive feet first into the softness of the first fallen blossom.

I feel excited, hopeful. There is a slow, soft blooming of joy deep inside my belly, but I cannot show it, for those who do not see the seasons like I do would snatch it from me and take it for their own if they even heard its whisper. For now, I must move slowly, softly turning my face to the sun just a little. Bowing my head in reverence to the deep darkness of winter, just a little more.

§

Come spring I decided to return. I have sat for four moons every night by my window, sending it all up in the air for the sky to take it. The warm rains came last month, they woke me in the middle of the night to tell me they were bringing it back for me, to me.

Today, on my early morning walk I saw the yellow medicine flowers gently blooming, and I heard myself whisper 'It is time'. I do not know what I will need when I get there, though I know what I need to do.

I take nothing but a spoon, a fresh jar, and a yard of yarn. Some stones in my pocket. Birdsong. This is enough for now.

§

We'd meet on Tuesdays. 'Pastry day' we'd call it. I'd pack up a fine basket of grains and linen and make my way swiftly to her, for 'baking'.

To anyone who's watching I am just a girl, off to see my teacher for classes:

How to fill a belly.
How to roast the finest bird.

They have no idea.

Once inside I shed my wares and promptly take my seat by the fire. There is work to do and we have so little time.

Out from her pantry she brings a selection of tiny, coloured, glass jars. Some bottles. We line them up neatly - each week a new one is added. I am to learn them all by name, and only then will she begin to tell me.

Today I have brought one for her - I found it in the square underneath the grain store water. It is blue. It feels like winter.

She takes it in her hand, running her old fingers up and down the smooth glass surface.

Holding it to my face, she smiles at me. I put it to my ear and listen.

§

Her words penetrated me - a piercing pain, with every story spoken.

A lone bird flew over the bleak mid-winter sky, and I find myself thinking about sewing and how I'd wasted so many years mending clothes when I could have been weaving webs and wonders.

I felt the sharpness of a needle between my finger and thumb. Looking at her, though she was talking of something else, she could see what I was doing.

'Show me' she said. 'I have never seen it done that way.'

I pulled the thread from my imaginary pocket - it is always full of treasures and somehow, I always find exactly what I need there, though I'd never let them search it of course. Today it is yellow - the spun hairs of an incoming spring, and a fine colour to craft a net to catch him with.

I pass one end to her. She grasps it gently, smiles at me - and we begin.

§

The sunlight danced over the water. Clouds passing slowly in a bluing sky. A ring of fire surfacing on the horizon. To the untrained eye it seemed a normal midsummer's morning - but the ravens above told a different story.

They have been watching this spot for lifetimes. And I have sat here with them, moon after moon, their black eyes seeing all, and their song singing a sullen tune that no one chose to hear. They come to me when there are messages I need to know from those that came before me - so now I visit almost daily as they call me in to listen.

I wonder - will they ever tell my story - and will I ever dare to too?

The wind picks up - the longest day has passed, and autumn is on the wind, unbeknown to the optimistic many signalling that winter is coming to us once again. I do not fear the seasons, for darkness has become my only ally in this work. In this life that I've been given.

I take the yellow summer flower I know as nature's medicine from under my skirt and slip it softly into my pocket. In the distance the boatman calls. Dawn is breaking. I rise to my feet gently and leave.

§

I pulled a ribbon for you, that day, right under the weeping willow tree, sat in the shade as the wind howled around us and I wondered how we'd got here.

Earlier, I planted a myrtle tree for you. Walked a thousand miles to get there with the wind at my back, saw the sun birth the moon as I took rest midway at the millhouse. It kept raining.

I picked a rose for you in the cottage garden - that place where time has no meaning and all that seems to matter are the water meadows.

I wished in the well for you, drew the water from the earth. Drank it, in blessing.

I stood on the land for you, returned for you, absorbed it all.

The cathedral bell tolled for you.

I wept for you.

Floated away for you.

You closed the door.

§

I am always finding ways to cross bridges. The middle is both a meeting and a letting go - a weaving of webs and untying of ribbons. Magic is found in the movement. It is made when we stand still, right in the centre.

I arrived sooner than I imagined I would, for I have always been the last to show - so it was as much a surprise to me as it was to them.

I had readied the space to receive them, and prepared myself with what I needed to be able to serve. This part of my doing is so familiar, and I have come to know it very well. It even shows up in my dreams if I'm lucky - it really is a lifelong, lifewide journey. Of course the birds have gathered too - they always do and as ever they are here before me. They will stay until long after I am gone.

§

We have gathered for the last time in this way, but he says there will be more. As the embers of the winter hearth burn low, he speaks of summer, and a season for rest and making. Long, kind days will nurture all sorts of things that the long years have not, and hope brings a certain kind of lightness to even the darkest story.

He is writing too. The manuscripts he makes are a version of those I do, but he brings a depth to the picture that only a man who's travelled as far as him can. He has been birthing this for lifetimes - I wonder what stars he took down from the night sky of the Holy Land and how he will weave what he gathered there and kept safe for so long in to the heart of this story. I wonder about the walnut in his pocket too and what that has seen and known from inside the earth up and out. It is dark for a reason and can tell a thousand tales bone deep, in tongues and in whispers. It is clear that it is time to listen. These fruits are ready to ripen now.

What I have to say is different from him, though it is all connected. We speak of the same time and place from different sides of the story - a warp and weft crafted from a shared, ancient loom. There is a coming together in the yarn of it and the magic is made in the middle it seems - spinning has always woven the finest textured silk and I am very good at that.

So I have said I will return, in fact I have made it clear I must. There is a seat round this fire that is mine for the taking and has been named so for all time. I will bring my papers with me and dive deep in to the crafting in this circle. Someone else is coming who knows the ways too, I do not know them yet, but they have been here on this river and have visited the well. They are charged with solid work - bringing gold thread with them to match with my silver - stitching this into a fine and sacred story, readying it to journey through the water.

Weavers Weaving

Silver Apple Branches

§

Sometimes it is so complicated there is no way to digest it all, and all the ways I know how come tumbling down around me as the earth crumbles under foot and the sky slides open.

So I look away, eyes wide open - but soft, a periphery - and wait for it to come in to view.

§

I call you here to meet the darkness
To come to the shadows
The edges
To know yourself here
The fullness of you
In storms and stillness and weeping, all salt, bones and seeing.
Sky above, Earth below
A shiver
A memory

And you, the knowing.

I ask you to meet yourself here
To hear your own sacred call

The echo

(The echo)

I ask you to go beyond
To listen softly
Whispers
A drum beat
To come back
To stand in the centre
To breathe deep
To remember
To stay.

§

Some days I pretend to be here as I sit still, here on this bench in my body.

To those watching I'm simply a woman waiting. A girl even. Inconspicuous. Nothing to do, nothing to see here.

What they've never realised is that I put my body here on this bench every day and slip straight out of it, leaving it there whilst I slide down to the river to listen and to learn. Whilst I head to the water to pray.

§

I turned to see a wise old bird right next to me. I had taken some leaves to the river and somehow without me knowing, it had gotten there. It stands stone still, eyes wide, watching, waiting. I daren't move. It is a giant, on one leg, wings wide wide open.

An old lady passes by, she tells me she will tread softly. I don't know if she talks to me or the bird. Neither of us seems to notice and in the enforced quiet she makes so much noise. I hear my heart beating, feel it in my throat.

I wonder if he's on his way yet. I sense he might be, and I want to be there ready to warm the hearth for him when he comes home.

The bird is still waiting. Frozen. It watches over something, unknown but felt deeply, just like I do. I have been holding my breath this whole time. It knows and it cares not. I wish that I could say the same. The eve is drawing close. The sky has turned the strangest colour, a storm is brewing but I know not what it means. I must go now for I am weary and need rest.

§

They say the rain wakes them, but the heavier it comes the more it sends me straight in to a different kind of slumber. I rise out of my body at the first drops of it and leave it there, not returning until the morning - daybreak is my call.

I travel far. This journey is a returning - a blessed invocation.

§

She is a woman of many faces. The scene in front of me is so busy. It seems an ordinary day in the city - clamour and chaos, colour, buttons, bridges and bears. And so so many birds, waiting to cross so many bridges. There are men here too and women, so many women, waiting to slip off their skin and return to the river.

I sit here looking, watching as if I'm not in it, as if they aren't me, but of course it is real and they are, because I too know birds and rivers. I too know how to cross bridges. I too know how to wear the skin of another, to stop anyone from seeing, to stop them from knowing - from saying my real name.

So, I perch here, to the side of this picture, out of view to most except a certain few. I am not the centre of this story.

§

To hide is to wait without courage. To feel shame and shadow so tightly that the cave of our lives is a prison - shackles, breathless.

I am to learn from this I know.

But the cave is calling. I am being beckoned and as I stand here at the doorway, I know I refuse to go in to that place that's mine (my mother always said I was an obstinate child).

So, I will light the fire, call the shapes from the darkness. Invite them to the threshold here with me. The space between heartbeats.

§

The sun enveloped us - and all I could feel was a deep sense of fear for the loss of my own shadow.

My shadow, you see, is the only part of me I've ever really known. The only part of me that has any sort of clue what it's doing and what's really going on around here.

We have known each other for lifetimes - lifetimes upon lifetimes, and we have travelled every step of every path together. So, when the sun enveloped us I smiled at you all - staring wide-eyed smiling at me, slipped out of my skin and left my shell playing there with you in the garden.

The rest of me slithered out amongst the slightly overgrown grass, whilst everyone around me cooed distractedly at the season's first bloom of roses, and slipped down to the banks of the river to search.

§

There was movement in my soul that day, as I sat in the fresh late spring of the wispy ancient forest, where years had passed since the people who had planted the first rose bushes had left that garden. The alchemy and the wisdom had been brewing for days, blowing around us, floating on whispers and refusing to take root for any length of time.

We walked down the crooked path as the ground began to stir and get whipped in to a frenzy. Looking in from the outside you'd see strolling, companionship and gentle inquiry, but inside the cogs had turned and welcomed the tempest, a full change of direction, never to return again.

We crossed the threshold. The stars burning on the stone-cold walls as we watched them. I wonder who placed them there and whether when they did, they had any idea that they would light the way to such redemption.

I look at them and see the red light in their eyes. I think it must have been the faer folk that did it. And here we are in ceremony, shapeshifters, and black dogs, the lot of them.

§

I can see he is so very angry and though every part of my body wants to run away, because I've been taught to do so, I find myself running headlong into him - and by default into it all.

There is no place like home, and I've been searching for this shade of blue my whole life, diving into the heart of every picture to find it, scouring the sky and scrying the water, just to see it briefly. But I know I can never hold it in my hand, for if I tried to, it would deny me. Many flowers bloom here.

§

Don't love me the way they always told you it should be - soft and warm and yielding, tender. Love me fiercely. Love me with fire - with straight lines and hard edges.

Love my darkness, love the parts of me that others cannot or daren't see.

Love me enough to eat me. Not because I'm sweet or moreish, but because you're addicted. Crave my bitter, salty, lingering taste - the one you cannot shift and would fight for, kill for, die for.

Don't love me for lifetimes, love me for the ending, for the knowing that death will come to all of us - and for the knowledge that I'll be the last thought in your mind - the last breath on your lips as you cross that line.

§

She is wise, so she has taken your knives.

She will call you to her when she is ready, when it is time, and you will know because the clocks will stop turning. Clouds will pass over the blue skies above you. Time will stand still - your life unfurling, everything a memory and you'll run towards her as your heart skips a beat and the chains that bind you fall to set you free.

You will leap into her arms as your breath freezes over - a thousand whispers crossing your ice-cold lips as the world turns upside down, your belly in your mouth, you eating your words as you split wide open onto the pavement, regretting every minute of the days when you chose to hate loving her.

§

I went there last week, and they'd clearly been, because everything had moved, and nothing was how I'd left it. I wondered if it was the wind that had taken things, but the minute I sat, I felt it.

I wonder how they knew. Whether someone had seen me, visiting day after day, and gone out of their way to tell them. I'd taken great care to come at different times, in guises - perhaps even that had drawn their eye. I will retreat to my cloak for the rest of winter and think up other plans for the light time. Blending in has never been my thing but I have learned to be ether when needed, and now that happens more than ever, so I will keep finding ways to move and know.

I'm here again now, early morning. I look at two men sitting close by, deep in conversation about the land they tend, and how they do it. Nobody bats an eyelid, but if I or any other women stop to join in, they will. They are right in the spot where I like to meet her and show no signs of moving. I listen softly, then look away for a moment, my thoughts lost in the river. Three boys have taken their place in an instant - again they are sitting. Of course they are guarding, in a way that no one, except those that really dare to look could tell. I am mad that I missed their movement, but such is the way it seems, and this is a season of patience - and a season for sharpening skill.

I watch from the outside, where mostly it's safest. A man wrapped in black moves in now, a small girl by his side, watching too. I look at her and wonder, will it ever be any different? She cries and he shushes her - we all know the answer, but I pray in whispers that something else is coming, and I am ready to step in.

The birds on the water are restless, the trees ever impatient. Connected. The sky says that spring is ready to break through and with that will come a turning. A swan flies overhead, low enough to almost touch it. A crow drops in, like a stone, to remind me, and to mark the spot until I return.

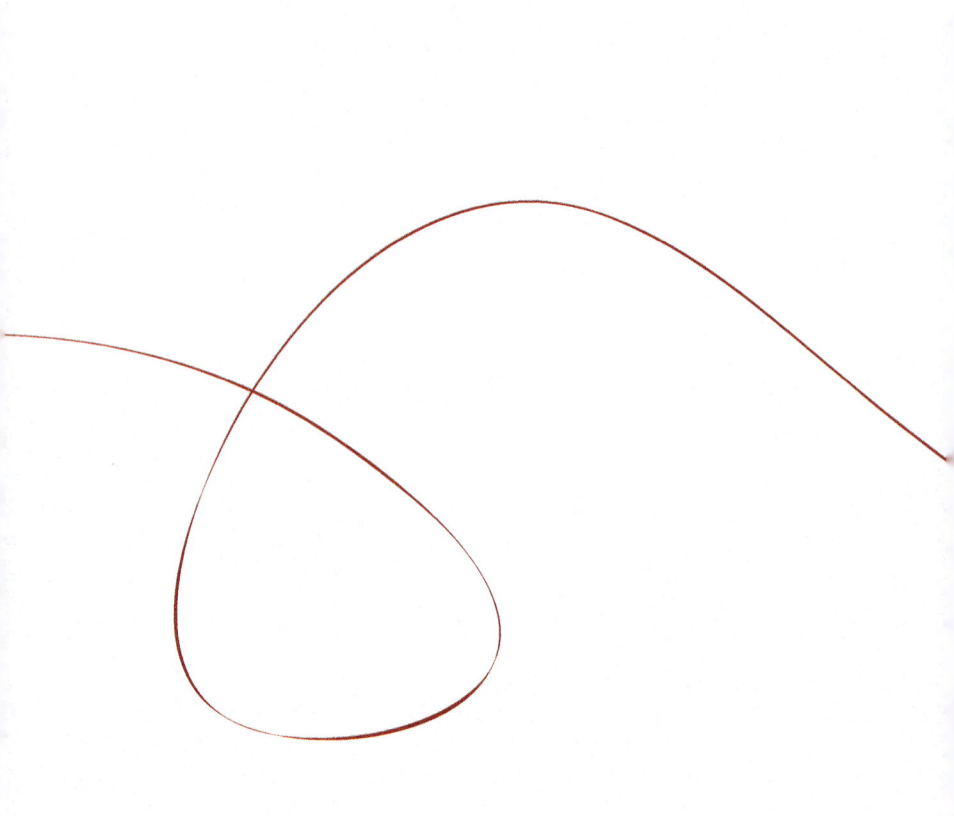

Epilogue

I made a prayer for you today
Stitched it out of the fabric of my being
Washed it
Pressed it
Folded it neatly in to tiny, careful creases
Then gave it away to the wind for you to take it.

I drank an offering for you today
Bowl by bowl
Hot water scalding my lips, each bitter sip a benediction.

I walked a pilgrimage for you today
Every step on the damp earth a confession, a blessing
Each leaf a sermon from you to me
All the lessons you never gave me
All the autumns I wish you'd stayed.

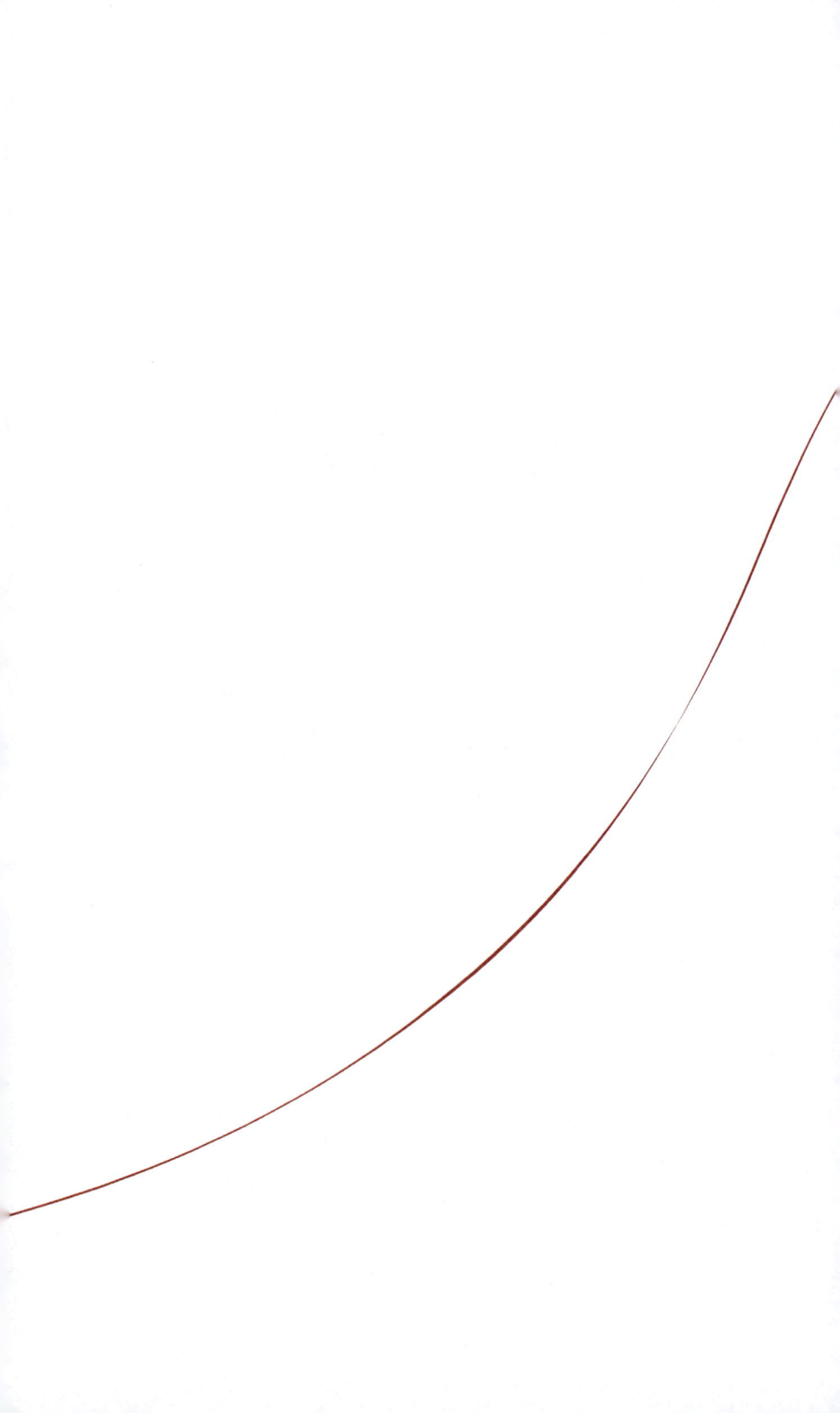

*Thank you for travelling with us -
please take this wisdom, and use it well*

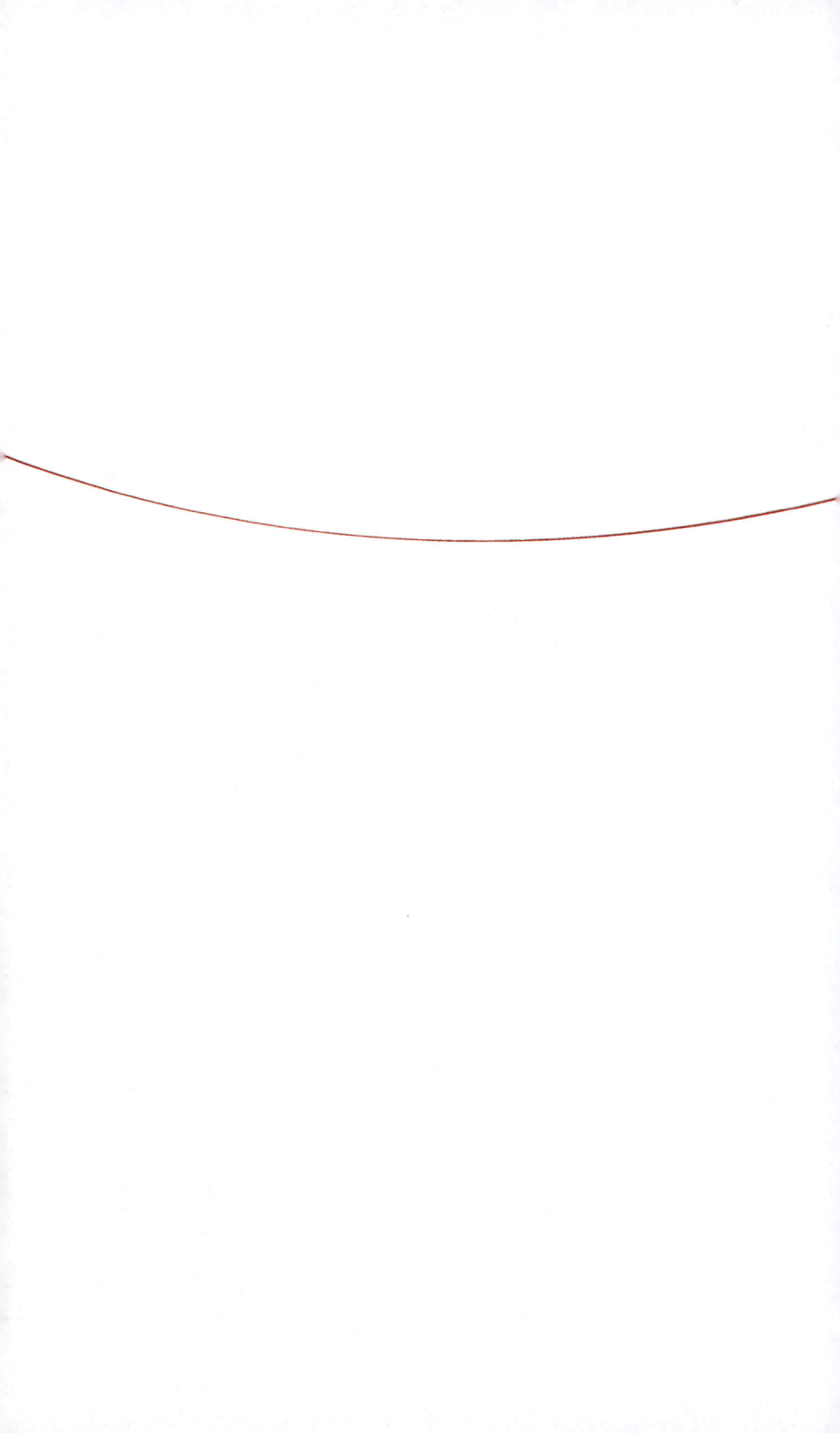